21st Century Junior Library

Visit the Dentist!

by Katie Marsico

CHERRY LAKE PUBLISHING * ANN ARBOR, MICHIGAN

Published in the United States of America by Cherry Lake Publishing
Ann Arbor, Michigan
www.cherrylakepublishing.com

Content Adviser: John Toupin, DDS, Toupin Dental and Associates, Novi, MI

Reading Adviser: Marla Conn, ReadAbility, Inc

Photo Credits: © Claudia Paulussen/Shutterstock Images, cover; © Rob Marmion/Shutterstock Images, 4; © phetsamay philavanh/Shutterstock Images, 6; © Zurijeta/Shutterstock Images, 8; © Sergey Nivens/Shutterstock Images, 10; © Pavel L Photo and Video/Shutterstock Images, 12; © Kirill Link/Shutterstock Images, 14; © Dragon Images/Shutterstock Images, 16; © BlueSkyImage/Shutterstock Images, 18; © N. Mitchell/Shutterstock Images, 20

LIBRARY OF CONGRESS CATALOGING-IN-PUBLICATION DATA

Marsico, Katie, 1980- author.
 Visit the dentist! / by Katie Marsico.
     pages cm. – (Your healthy body)
 Includes bibliographical references and index.
 ISBN 978-1-63188-986-8 (hardcover)—ISBN 978-1-63362-025-4 (pbk.)—ISBN 978-1-63362-064-3 (pdf)—ISBN 978-1-63362-103-9 (ebook)
 1. Dentistry—Juvenile literature. 2. Dentists—Juvenile literature. I. Title.
 RK63.M3682 2015
 617.6–dc23   2014021525

Cherry Lake Publishing would like to acknowledge the work of
The Partnership for 21st Century Skills.
Please visit www.p21.org *for more information.*

Printed in the United States of America
Corporate Graphics

CONTENTS

5 Does That Smile Shine?

11 The Dental Exam

17 What Does the Dentist Do?

22 Glossary

23 Find Out More

24 Index

24 About the Author

Even if you don't have a dentist appointment, it's always important to brush your teeth!

Does That Smile Shine?

Lynn decides to brush one more time before she visits Dr. Wilson, the family dentist. The last time she saw him was six months ago. She tries to take care of

Think!

Think about the last time you visited the dentist. What do you remember about your examination, or checkup? Did you feel nervous before your appointment? How about after it?

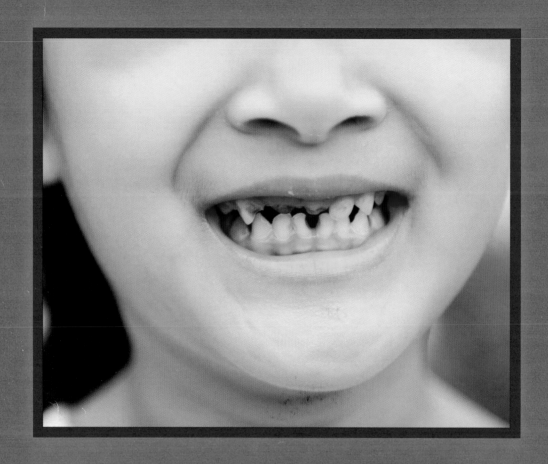

Teeth that aren't properly cared for often turn brown, break, or fall out.

her teeth and gums. But she's still a little nervous. What if she has a **cavity**?

People depend on their teeth, jaws, and gums to eat, speak, and smile. That's why it's important to practice good dental **hygiene**. Many healthy dental habits involve preventing **plaque** buildup.

Make a Guess!

How many teeth are in your mouth? Can you guess? Most 3-year-olds have a set of 20 baby teeth. These teeth start falling out 2 to 3 years later. They are slowly replaced by **permanent** teeth. You should have 28 permanent teeth by the time you're 13 years old.

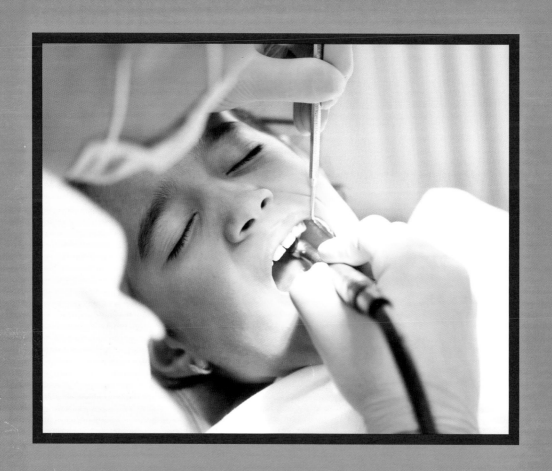

A dental hygienist is the person who cleans and counts your teeth.

Bacteria react with sugar found in foods. This forms acid that wears away tooth **enamel** and forms cavities. Plaque also leads to gingivitis. This disease causes painful, swollen gums.

Brushing teeth is one way to prevent cavities and gingivitis. Other ways are flossing and avoiding sugary foods and drinks. These everyday activities help support dental health.

So does visiting a dentist at least twice a year. It's a good opportunity to ask questions.

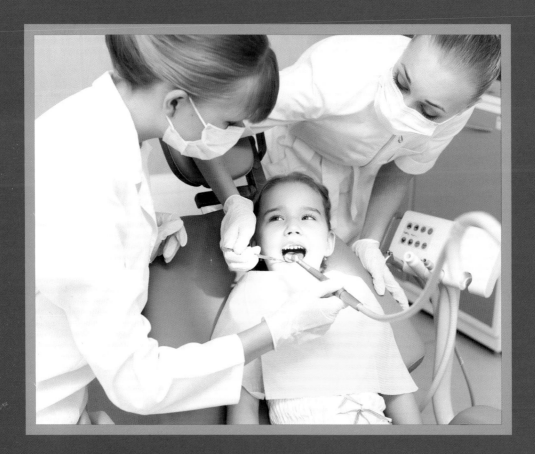

Dental workers are trained to use many tools.

The Dental Exam

It's time for a closer look at Lynn's teeth! Ms. Cortez is the **dental hygienist**. She walks Lynn to the exam room and asks how school is going.

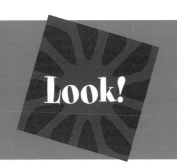

Look! Look at this picture of a dental exam. Why do you think the hygienist is wearing a mask and gloves? Why is the patient wearing a paper bib? What else do you notice?

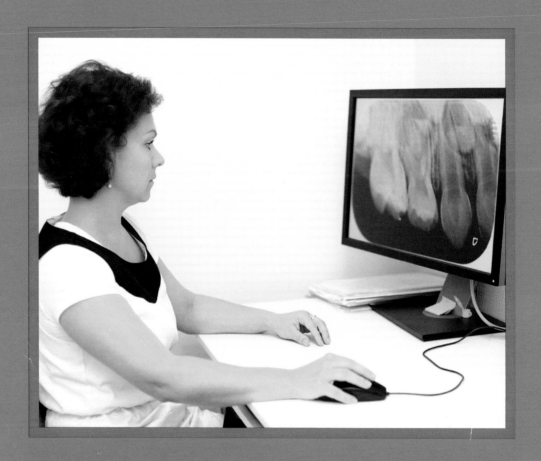

X-rays show dentists things they can't see from just looking in your mouth.

Lynn sits in a large chair that leans back. Ms. Cortez switches on a bright overhead light. She asks Lynn to open wide! Ms. Cortez uses a mirror to examine her mouth.

Ms. Cortez counts Lynn's teeth and takes a few **x-rays**. These photographs will help Dr. Wilson spot any hidden cavities or gum problems. Ms. Cortez shows Lynn what instruments she'll use to clean and polish her teeth. One is an electric toothbrush. Ms. Cortez lets Lynn choose either cotton candy or bubblegum toothpaste.

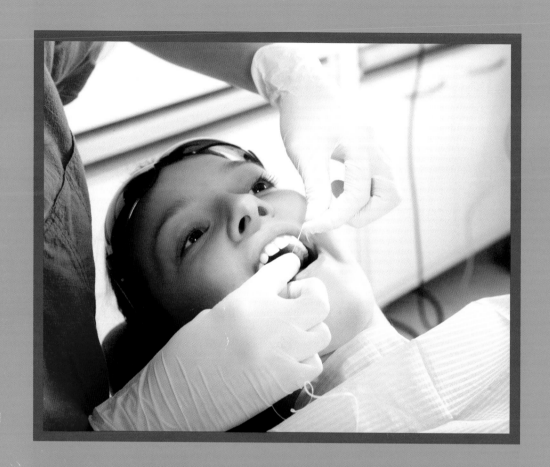

Flossing is a good way to reach the food
your toothbrush misses.

Ms. Cortez sprays water and air inside Lynn's mouth as she works. She uses a small **syringe** to do this. The water rinses Lynn's teeth. The air dries them. Ms. Cortez drains any leftover water and fluids such as **saliva**. She uses a suction tip to do this. This instrument is made from a small plastic tube attached to a hose. Ms. Cortez finishes by flossing Lynn's teeth. The dental exam is almost over.

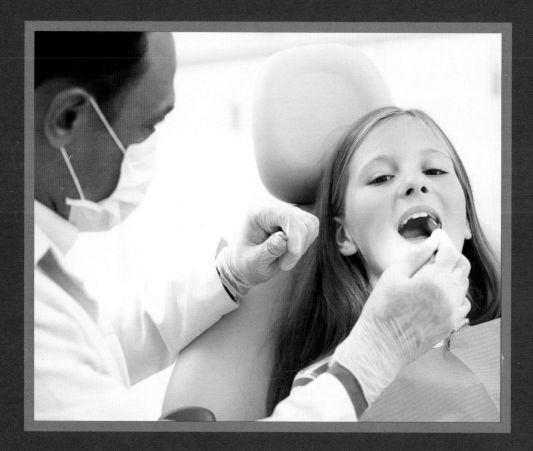

A dentist uses a tiny mirror to look
around your mouth.

What Does the Dentist Do?

Ms. Cortez tells Lynn to sit for just a little longer. Dr. Wilson and Lynn's mom come into the exam room.

Ask Questions!

What clues do dentists look for as they search for cavities? How do they treat the cavities they find? Ask your dentist to help answer these questions.

The dentist might give you some new dental supplies and show you how to use them.

Dr. Wilson asks Lynn to open her mouth once more. He uses the mirror to examine her teeth and gums.

He also checks Lynn's bite, to see how her top and bottom jaws work together. If they are crooked, she might need braces. He says all her teeth are lined up correctly. She doesn't have any cavities either!

Dr. Wilson tells Lynn to brush her teeth at least twice a day for 2 to 3 minutes each time. She should brush more than just the

If you follow your dentist's tips, you'll have
a healthy mouth and a bright smile!

front of her mouth. It's important to clean the back and side teeth, too.

Dr. Wilson wants Lynn to floss every day. He asks her to come back for another checkup in 6 months. Ms. Cortez hands Lynn a treat bag containing a toothbrush, toothpaste, floss, and sugar-free gum. Lynn knows she won't be nervous the next time she visits the dentist. Instead, she'll be prepared to show off her shining smile!

GLOSSARY

bacteria (bak-TEER-ee-uh) simple organisms that sometimes cause disease

cavity (KAH-vuh-tee) a hole in a tooth that is caused by decay, or rot

dental hygienist (DEN-tuhl hye-JEEN-ist) a person who works with a dentist and whose responsibilities include cleaning teeth

enamel (ih-NAH-muhl) a tooth's hard outer layer

hygiene (HYE-jeen) a group of habits people practice to stay healthy and clean

permanent (PUR-muh-nuhnt) meant to last for a long time

plaque (PLACK) a layer of bacteria that builds on teeth

saliva (suh-LYE-vuh) spit, or liquid produced in a person's mouth

syringe (suh-RINJ) an instrument made from a hollow tube attached to a needle

x-rays (EKS-rayz) images of teeth and bones created by a machine that produces powerful, invisible rays

FIND OUT MORE

BOOKS

Minden, Cecilia. *Dentists*. Mankato, MN: The Child's World, 2014.

Sateren, Shelley Swanson, and Mary Sullivan (illustrator). *Max and Zoe at the Dentist*. Minneapolis: Picture Window Books, 2012.

Silverstein, Alvin, Virginia Silverstein, and Laura Silverstein Nunn. *Handy Healthy Guide to Your Teeth*. Berkeley Heights, NJ: Enslow Publishers, Inc., 2014.

WEB SITES

KidsHealth—Going to the Dentist
kidshealth.org/kid/feel_better /people/go_dentist.html
Find out more about what happens during a dental exam, and get links to other articles on dental health.

Nova Scotia Dental Association—Healthy Teeth
healthyteeth.org
Test your knowledge of dental health with an online quiz and take a virtual tour of a dentist's office!

INDEX

B
bacteria, 9
bite, 19
braces, 19

C
cavities, 7, 9,
 13, 17

D
dental hygienist,
 8, 11–15
dentists, 16,
 17–21

E
enamel, 9
exam, dental,
 11–16

F
flossing, 9, 14,
 15, 21

G
gingivitis, 9
gums, 9, 13, 19

J
jaws, 19

M
mirror, 13, 16,
 19

P
plaque, 7, 9,
 13

S
saliva, 15
sugars, 9

T
teeth

X
x-rays, 12, 13

brushing, 4,
 5, 9, 19
cleaning, 8
examining,
 19
how many
 we have,
 7

ABOUT THE AUTHOR

Katie Marsico is the author of more than 150 children's books. She lives in a suburb of Chicago, Illinois, with her husband and children.